SHAPEDBYSCRIPTURE

In the Beginning

GENESIS
1-11

ALEX VARUGHESE

Copyright © 2019 by The Foundry Publishing
The Foundry Publishing
PO Box 419527
Kansas City, MO 64141
thefoundrypublishing.com

978-0-8341-3761-5

Printed in the
United States of America

Cover Design: J.R. Caines
Interior Design: J.R. Caines
Layout: Mike Williams

The internet addresses, email addresses, and phone numbers in this book are
accurate at the time of publication. They are provided as a resource. The Foundry
Publishing does not endorse them or vouch for their content or permanence.

10 9 8 7 6 5 4 3 2 1

Contents

THE *SHAPED BY SCRIPTURE* SERIES

The first step of an organized study of the Bible is the selection of a biblical book, which isn't always an easy task. Often people pick a book they are already familiar with, or books they think will be easy to understand, or books that, according to popular opinion, seem to have more relevance to Christians today than other books of the Bible. However, it is important to recognize the truth that God's Word is not limited to just a few books. All the biblical books, both individually and collectively, communicate God's Word to us. As Paul affirms in 2 Timothy 3:16, "All Scripture is God-breathed and is useful for teaching, rebuking, correcting and training in righteousness." We interpret the term "God-breathed" to mean inspired by God. If Christians are going to take 2 Timothy 3:16 seriously, then we should all set the goal of encountering God's Word as communicated through all sixty-six books of the Bible. New Christians or those with little to no prior knowledge of the Bible might find it best to start with a New Testament book like 1 John, James, or the Gospel of John.

By picking up this volume, you have chosen to study the book of Genesis. You've made a great choice because this first book of the Bible lays a foundation for the rest of the story of God. Because the goal of this series is to illustrate an appropriate method of studying the Bible, instead of a comprehensive study of the entire book, our study will be limited to a few select passages in Genesis. In this volume, we will focus on seven stories taken from chapters 1–11. We will take up another set of seven stories from chapters 12–50 in the second volume of our study of Genesis.

How This Study Works

This Bible study is intended for a period of seven weeks. We have chosen a specific passage for each week's study. This study can be done individually or with a small group.

For individual study, we recommend a five-day study each week, following the guidelines given below:

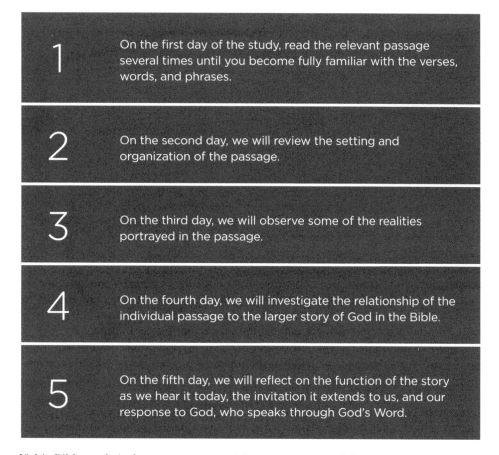

1 On the first day of the study, read the relevant passage several times until you become fully familiar with the verses, words, and phrases.

2 On the second day, we will review the setting and organization of the passage.

3 On the third day, we will observe some of the realities portrayed in the passage.

4 On the fourth day, we will investigate the relationship of the individual passage to the larger story of God in the Bible.

5 On the fifth day, we will reflect on the function of the story as we hear it today, the invitation it extends to us, and our response to God, who speaks through God's Word.

If this Bible study is done as a group activity, we recommend that members of the group meet together on the sixth day to share and discuss what they have learned from God's Word and how it has transformed their lives.

You may want to have a study Bible to give you additional insights as we work through the book of Genesis. Another helpful resource is *Discovering the Old Testament*, available from The Foundry Publishing.

Literary Forms in the Bible

There are several literary forms represented throughout the Bible. The divinely inspired writers used various techniques to communicate God's Word to their ancient audiences. The major literary forms (also known as genres) of the Bible are:

- narratives

- laws

- history

- Wisdom literature (in the form of dialogues and proverbial statements)

- poetry (consisting of poems of praise, lament, trust in God, and more)

- prophecy

- discourses

- parables

- miracle stories

- letters (also known as epistles)

- exhortations

- apocalyptic writings

Within each of these forms, one may find subgenres. Each volume in the *Shaped by Scripture* series will briefly overview the genres found in the book of the Bible that is the subject of that study.

When biblical writers utilized a particular literary form, they intended for it to have a specific effect on their audience. This concept can be understood by examining genres that are familiar to us in our contemporary setting. For example, novels that are comedies inspire good and happy feelings in their readers; tragedies, on the other hand, are meant to induce sorrow. What is true of the intended effect of literary forms in contemporary literature is also true of literary forms found in the Bible.

THE BOOK OF GENESIS

The message of the biblical books, though it originates with God, comes to us through individuals whom God inspired to communicate his word to humanity. They fulfilled their task by utilizing their literary skill as speakers and writers of God's message. This message came to these individuals in particular circumstances in the history of God's people—the Israelites in the Old Testament period, and the early Christian church in the first century AD. In addition, biblical books communicate certain clearly developed understandings about God, humanity, sin, judgment, salvation, human hope, and more. Bible studies should be done with an awareness of the theological themes in a particular book. So, prior to our engagement with the actual text of Genesis, we shall briefly summarize what we know about the authorship of Genesis, literary forms found in the book, the historical setting of the book and that of its writing, the literary structure of the book, and its major theological themes.

Who Wrote Genesis?

The book of Genesis belongs to a collection of five biblical books that are known as the Pentateuch in the Jewish tradition. They can also be called the Five Books, the Five Scrolls, the Law, or the Torah. In addition to Genesis, the collection includes Exodus, Leviticus, Numbers, and Deuteronomy. Some scholars hold to the ancient Jewish and Christian view of these books as the work of Moses, but others think it is possible that they have multiple authors. Genesis is a collection of Israel's oral traditions about creation and the beginning of human history; and about Abraham, Isaac, and Jacob—the three foremost ancestors of the people group that later came to be called Israel. Though the authorship of Genesis and many other biblical books is frequently debated among Christians, we believe in the integrity of the biblical books as we find them in the Bible today.

Literary Form

The book of Genesis is considered narrative. It is written mostly in prose and is made up of stories. In chapters 1–11, the narrative focus is on creation and humanity as a whole. From chapters 12–50, we read the stories of the family of Abraham, Isaac, and Jacob. These stories deal with events that have taken place in the history of this family and the interactions of its various members with those within their family as well as outsiders. As a result of this familial focus, most of the stories in chapters 12–50 belong to a subcategory called *family stories* – in which a prominent individual plays a key role as the main character. In addition to the stories, Genesis also contains genealogical lists (in chapters 5, 10, 25, 36, and 46) that indicate the ancestries of various groups of people who once lived in the ancient world.

Entering the Story

Stories in Genesis (and in the rest of the Bible) are intended to draw readers into the various scenes portrayed in them. In other words, biblical stories are never meant to remain ancient stories, and readers are never meant to be detached from them. Reading a Genesis story is like being in a stadium and watching an exciting game. Very rarely do we see people at sporting events remain in the bleachers, unemotional and detached from the game. Most sports fans see themselves as part of the team, cheering victories and yelling at the players when they fail to execute the game plan. Likewise, the writers of Genesis invite us to enter into the story and become part of it. When we do, we soon discover that most of the narratives portray realities very much like those that exist in our world today. We find in the biblical characters reflections of our imperfect relationships, our doubts, our mistrust of God or others, our pride, our self-reliance, our violence, our family quarrels and rivalries, our cheating and deception, our hatred or mistreatment of others who are not like us. Even the few individuals we find in Genesis who demonstrate great personal integrity have character flaws.

Entering into a Genesis story and seeing ourselves and our own world through the lens of that story does not mean that the intended effect of the story has been accomplished entirely. Most of the Genesis stories relate to some crisis. In Genesis, we often find God entering into the midst of human crisis and addressing the characters in order to give instructions for resolving the crisis. When God's involvement is not directly reported in a particular story, we usually find it in preceding stories about the same character. Just like the people we know in real life, some of the characters in Genesis respond to God's voice and resolve their crisis; others do not.

The stories in Genesis accomplish their intended effect when readers respond to the invitation, or the challenge, they encounter inside the stories. The characters we meet in Genesis and their interactions with a faithful God motivate us to think of or imagine the alternative to our own crisis-ridden lives. How would a Genesis story change if the characters listened to God and took action to promote the healing of broken relationships and the well-being of others around them? How would our world look today if we did the same?

Genesis stories invite us to enter into and embrace the world God intended for us to live when God brought forth creation. We find the perfect model for such existence in the life of Jesus in the New Testament Gospels. By following the example of Jesus, and through our faith in him, we become God's new creation in the world. When we do this, and become what God originally created us to be, then we can say that the Genesis stories have had their intended effect. Personal transformation is the final effect intended by the stories in Genesis. In this way of reading and studying, we see the stories in Genesis extending beyond their ancient context and becoming God's living Word to us today!

This is the method of reading and studying the Bible we will follow in this book. We admit that this method is somewhat different from many popular Bible study materials and methods found in the marketplace today. Most of them seek to lay out theological, moral, ethical principles that can be derived from the stories and then applied to our life situations today. Without denying the merit of these types of resources, we suggest instead that life transformation, instead of life application, should be the goal of a Bible study—and transformation is, therefore, our goal in the *Shaped by Scripture* series.

Historical Context

We deal with two important and separate but related issues when we investigate the date and the historical context of Genesis (this is true of an investigation of all the biblical books). First, we examine the time and the particular context (historical, political, cultural, social, and religious) in which the stories of Genesis took place. Second, we examine the date and the context in which the book was actually composed by its editors/compilers. Both of these issues are important for us to consider. The former helps us to place specific stories in their particular setting, which is critical to our understanding of the realities portrayed in the stories. The latter helps us to discover how later generations would have heard and understood these stories.

Context of the Events in Genesis

Unfortunately, we cannot place the events in Genesis chapters 1–11 in a specific historical period because the events reported in them come from a period long before the documenting of history and civilization by humans began. We can only say that these events belong to the earliest period of human history and reflect the widely held beliefs of the Israelites about the origin of the world and humanity. They also set the context for the stories of Abraham, Isaac, and Jacob in chapters 12–50.

The stories in chapters 4–11 are filled with gaps. Though they are put together in a seamless fashion, we think the writers preserved only major incidents that changed the course of human history. For example, the writers cover the creation of the world through approximately 2000 BC in only eleven chapters. However, it takes them thirty-nine chapters (12–50) to tell the stories of Abraham, Isaac, and Jacob—the three great ancestors of the people who would later become the Israelites. This difference clearly suggests that the primary goal of the writers was to tell their own story.

Most scholars agree that these stories belong to the period of the Amorite civilization in Mesopotamia, Syria, and Palestine (roughly 2000–1700 BC). Scholars also believe that Abraham was part of a migratory movement of the Amorites from Mesopotamia into the Syria-Canaan region (see Genesis 11:27–32). The ancestors of the Israelites lived as seminomadic people who pitched their tents in places where they found pasture for their flock. They were not part of an organized religious group. They worshiped God by setting up altars and offering sacrifices. The head of the household carried out the priestly tasks.

Though Abraham himself once belonged to the polytheistic religion of the Amorites, his encounter with God led him to his belief in one true God, whom he called "Most High, Creator of heaven and earth" (Genesis 14:22). Scholars consider Abraham to be the founder of monotheism—belief in one God. Abraham, his son Isaac, and his grandson Jacob worshiped God by setting up altars in the places where God appeared to them during their travels.

Other than these sketchy details, we do not know much about the setting of the stories found in chapters 12–50.

Context of the Writing of Genesis

Most scholars believe that Genesis in its present form was written in the sixth century BC, when the Jewish people were living in exile in Babylon, after the Babylonians conquered Judah and brought an end to their political freedom in 586 BC. The exile threatened the future of the Jewish people and their identity as the covenant people of God in the world.

It is possible that the writer(s) of Genesis collected and compiled the oral stories from the past and put them together in written form with two goals in mind: (1) to provide the Jews in Babylon and future generations a foundational understanding of Israel's God as the creator and sustainer of the world; (2) to give the Jewish community a clear understanding of their identity and mission in the world—which understanding is that, though they are exiles, living away from the land God promised to their ancestors, they continue to be God's people. They belong to the family of Abraham, and they are a people with a mission to the world. The mission God gave to Abraham to be an instrument of God's blessing to all peoples on earth is their same, continued mission.

Investigating the context in which the books of the Bible were written is important when we hear God's Word today. Although the circumstances may differ, God's Word speaks today in our own life situations. So, although the details are different, we are able to experience Scripture in fresh and new ways. As we listen to the story of God in the Bible, we can experience God's Word as God's "living word" today.

Literary Structure

The fifty chapters in Genesis are organized under two major sections: chapters 1–11 contain several stories that deal with humanity as a whole. This section begins with two stories about God's creation of the world and humankind (chapters 1–2), followed by the story of humankind's first sin and the consequences that followed (chapter 3). The story of chapter 4 shows that violence has become a way of life in the world. Chapter 5 is a genealogical list that traces the ancestry of Noah, who is the main character in the story of the flood and who represents a new beginning for humanity in chapters 6–9. Chapter 10 is another genealogy that identifies the descendants of the three sons of Noah. Chapter 11 begins with another story of human rebellion against God and the consequence that followed, and ends with another genealogy that traces the ancestral line from Noah (through his son Shem) down to Terah and his better-known son Abraham (still known as Abram at this point).

Genesis chapters 12–50 contain the stories of Abraham, Isaac, and Jacob. Abraham stories are found from 12:1–25:18. Though Isaac's family is introduced in 25:19–34, we find him as the main hero only in the stories in chapter 26. The rest of the stories in Genesis (chapters 27–50) center on Jacob, who becomes the father of the twelve tribes of Israel. Though Joseph stories dominate chapters 37–50, Jacob remains in the background and plays a key role in the journey of the family from Canaan to Egypt, where they settle after the deaths of Jacob and Joseph. Thus, the stories in chapters 37–50 serve to set the scene for the book of Exodus, which begins with the story of Israel's centuries-long enslavement in Egypt.

Major Theological Themes

Genesis, though mostly filled with stories of families and individuals, contains many significant theological themes. The fact that Genesis begins with the account of God's creation of the world and everything in it leads us to surmise that the creation theme has a central place in the book. The following list shows how the various other themes in Genesis are connected to the creation theme.

Creation testifies to God's nature as a relational God. Through God's creation activities, God entered into a faithful relationship with God's creation (1:1–2:4).

Blessing is a fundamental way God relates to God's creation. God's blessing is the source of the growth and well-being of creation (1:22, 28; 2:3).

The God-given mission of human beings is to be God's image in the world. We do this through faithful relationship with God and with the rest of creation (1:26–28).

We are designated caretakers of creation. The authority God grants to humans is that of shepherds, not of despotic, exploitive, destructive rulers (1:26–28).

God created Sabbath rest. God's rest on the seventh day of creation models a work-rest rhythm for creation's existence (2:2–3).

Living in obedience to God is critical to faithful relationship with God (2:15–17).

Human beings failed to be God's image in the world. This failure resulted in a disruption of our relationship with God and with the rest of creation (3:1–24).

Sin through disobedience and rebellion against God became a destructive and pervasive reality in the world. God's judgment was the inevitable consequence of human sin (4:1–7:24).

 In the midst of the judgment of the flood, God remained gracious and created a new beginning for humanity through Noah and his family (6:9–9:17).

 Noah's descendants resisted God's mandate to spread over the entire earth. As a result, God's judgment came upon them (11:1–9; see also 1:28; 9:1).

 God entered into a special covenant relationship with Abraham. God promised to bless Abraham with numerous descendants and a land as their inheritance from God (12:1–3; 15:1–21; 17:1–27).

 God's promise of blessing to Abraham and his family (and all other human families) is an extension of God's blessing on creation (see 1:22, 28).

13

 God promised to bless "all peoples on earth" through Abraham (12:3). The mission of the covenant family was to be an instrument of God's blessing to others.

 Isaac and Jacob became the recipients of God's covenant promises to Abraham (26:1–6; 28:10–22).

 The future of Abraham and his family was shaped not only by the promises of God but also by their obedience to God (several stories in chapters 12–50 illustrate the obedient response of Abraham, Isaac, and Jacob to God's commands).

 God remained faithful to Joseph, a member of the covenant family, and surrounded him with God's presence during his trouble-filled days in Egypt (39:1–23).

Week One

GENESIS 1:1-2:3

Our purpose in studying the first chapters of Genesis is not to engage in speculative questions like when God created the world or whether the "day" referenced in the creation narrative is a literal, twenty-four-hour day. Nor will we engage in a creation-versus-evolution debate. We strongly believe that when we insist on needing certain answers to such questions, we miss the importance of receiving Scripture as the Word of God that God calls us to hear, and to which God invites us to respond.

The narrative in 1:1–2:3 is one of two stories of creation in the book of Genesis. The second story is found in 2:4–25. It is possible that the two creation stories (God creating the world in 1:1–2:3, and God making humankind and placing them in the garden in 2:4–25) may have existed independently of each other until they were put together and given their present form by the writer(s) of Genesis. Today, it is important to read both stories to gain a comprehensive understanding of creation.

Genesis 1:1–2:3 reveals the literary skill of the writer in various ways. The words and phrases in this story are precise and carefully chosen. We find in this story evidence of the writer's preference for the number seven and its multiples: the phrase "God saw . . . it was good" appears seven times; God is mentioned thirty-five times; earth is mentioned twenty-one times. It is a tightly knit-together story that utilizes a carefully planned structure. Scholars have noted the following pattern in the organization of this story:

1. Announcement ("And God said . . .").

2. God's command ("Let there be . . .").

3. Fulfillment of the command (". . . there was . . .").

4. God's evaluation ("God saw that it was good").

5. Seven-day structure ("There was evening, and there was morning—the first day," etc.).

The symmetrical arrangement of the six days of creation, as illustrated below, is further evidence of the literary skill of the writer(s) of this account:

DAY 1
(light)

DAY 2
(sky and sea)

DAY 3
(dry ground)

DAY 4
(lights in the sky)

DAY 5
(birds in the sky and
creatures in the sea)

DAY 6
(land animals
and humans)

WEEK 1, DAY 1

Listen to the story in Genesis 1:1–2:3 by reading it aloud several times until you become familiar with its verses, words, and phrases. Enjoy the experience of imagining the story in your mind, picturing each event as it unfolds.

WEEK 1, DAY 2
GENESIS 1:1–2:3

The Setting

It is customary to begin the study of a biblical story by asking questions about its historical, cultural, religious, and literary setting. Since Genesis 1:1–2:3 reports what Christians consider to be the first event in history, these questions are difficult to ask about this passage. Because the Bible does not speak of any prior activity of God, we let the events reported Genesis 1:1–2:3 serve as the foundational setting of all the events that follow throughout the rest of Genesis as well as the rest of the Bible. Therefore, when we read any other story in the Bible, we interpret it through the lens of this creation story. We will then be able to discover whether that story upholds the theological claims made in the creation story.

Abraham's faith in God as the creator became the beginning point of the Israelites' faith traditions (see Genesis 14:22). In Genesis 1:1–2:3, we find the inspired writer's clear articulation of Israel's faith that elevates the God of Israel as the supreme creator of heaven and earth. Most scholars think the actual writing of this account took place in the sixth century BC, during the exile of the Jews (Israelites) in Babylon.

The Plot

To discover the plot of Genesis 1, let's first look at the way the story is structured by its writer. These verses are a carefully developed story of creation; the writer leaves several clues to help the readers recognize its arrangement. We will discover them as we engage this story. For the purpose of our study, we divide this story into eleven paragraphs. Let's examine each of those eleven paragraphs. **Below, write down next to each grouping of verses the main event or theme those verses report (follow the pattern provided for 1:1–2, 3–5, 26–28; 2:2–3).**

1. Genesis 1:1–2
God created the heavens and the earth; the earth didn't have any form, and everything was dark.

2. Genesis 1:3–5
God created light and separated the light from the darkness.

3. Genesis 1:6–8

_____

_____

4. Genesis 1:9–10

_____

_____

5. Genesis 1:11–13

_____

_____

6. Genesis 1:14–19

_____

_____

7. Genesis 1:20–23

_____

_____

8. Genesis 1:24–25

_____

_____

9. Genesis 1:26–28

God created humankind in God's image and placed them as rulers over the earth and over all

non-human creatures.

10. Genesis 1:29–2:1

_____

_____

11. Genesis 2:2–3

God rested on the seventh day, blessed it, and made it holy.

_____

WORD STUDY NOTES #1

[1] God is always the subject of the verb "created" (*bara'*) in the Old Testament; thus, the Hebrew form of the word we translate as "create" denotes an action only God can perform.

[2] "Formless and empty" (*tohu vavohu*) portrays the earth's condition as desert-like or unproductive and vacant; the Hebrew noun *tohu* also reflects a condition that lacks order.

[3] "Darkness" in verse 2 is simply the absence of light.

[4] "The Spirit of God" (*ruach 'elohim*) refers here to the powerful presence of God. The phrase "hovering over" is meant to bring to mind something like a mother bird hovering over her nest to protect her fledglings.

WORD STUDY NOTES #2

[1] The word "good" here is not the opposite of evil; it simply conveys God's assessment that what God created will perform its intended function.

What's Happening in the Story?

As we notice certain circumstances in the story, we will begin to see how they are similar to or different from the realities of our world. The story will become the lens through which we see the world in which we live today. In our study today, you may encounter words and/or phrases that are unfamiliar to you. Some of the particular words and translation choices for them have been explained in more detail in the **Word Study Notes**. If you are interested in even more help or detail, you can supplement this study with a Bible dictionary or other Bible study resource.

1. Genesis 1:1–2

The story begins with the writer's affirmation that what we see above ("the heavens") and what we see around us ("the earth") are created[1] by God. The author describes the condition of the earth as unproductive and vacant.[2] Moreover, the earth was covered by the waters ("the deep"). Verse 2 also says that "darkness"[3] loomed over the surface of the waters. Verse 2 concludes with the picture of this desolate and dark condition of the earth under the powerful, caring, and protective presence of God.[4]

2. Genesis 1:3–5

Light appears as God commands. Here we see the first of the nine instances of "And God said" in this story (see vv. 6, 9, 11, 14, 20, 24, 26, 29). Verse 4 says that God sees and calls the light "good."[1] God repeats this evaluation six more times throughout the chapter (see vv. 10, 12, 18, 21, 25, and 31). Verse 4 also shows a world where light and darkness are separated by God so that day and night have their existence in separate times and spheres. The naming of the light and the darkness as "day" and "night" indicates that they have divinely assigned functions to carry out in creation. The references to "evening," "morning," and "the first day" place God's creation activities within time as we know it (see the repetition of this statement in vv. 8, 13, 19, 23, and 31).

3. Genesis 1:6–8

God gives a command ("let there be a vault"), announces God's intention ("to separate water from water"), then proceeds to make the vault ("sky"), and separates the waters that cover the entire surface of the earth. The naming of the vault conveys its divinely assigned function. The scene portrayed of the sky here is that of a bowl set upside down on the earth with water both above and beneath it.[1]

Practice the above pattern to jot down a summary description of the world and reality that is portrayed in verses 9–10.

4. Genesis 1:9–10

_____

_____

_____

_____

5. Genesis 1:11–13

The land responds to God's command and produces seed-bearing plants and fruit-bearing trees. Here we find the first signs of life appearing on the earth. These plants and trees are not all alike; they belong to a variety of different kinds, or groups.

6. Genesis 1:14–19

God gives a command ("let there be lights in the vault of the sky") and delegates certain tasks ("separate the day from the night," "serve as signs to mark sacred times, and days and years," "to give light on the earth"). God then proceeds to make "two great lights," the "greater" one to rule the day and the "lesser" one to rule the night. God also places stars in the sky. The scene thus presents these heavenly bodies as God's direct creation. They exist to carry out the functions God assigned to them.

WORD STUDY NOTES #3

[1] The ancient readers of this story would have understood the water above the vault as the source of rain, snow, and other forms of precipitation (see Genesis 7:11–12; 8:2; Job 38:22–41).

You don't have to have a master's degree in biblical scholarship or languages to learn to think about the text in a way that helps you both understand the words and imagine the bigger reality behind them.

19

7. Genesis 1:20–23

Animal life appears for the first time. God creates living creatures to inhabit the space of the sea and birds to occupy the earth and the space above the earth. We see here only a very general portrait of the creatures that inhabit the sea ("great creatures of the sea and every living thing with which the water teems"). God who creates also blesses creation in the very first instance of God's blessing we find in the Bible. The divine blessing endows the sea creatures and the birds with the capacity to populate the seas and the earth. This particular blessing ("be fruitful and increase in number") is also a command to participate with God in the continuation of God's creational activities.

Create your own brief description of the world/reality portrayed in verses 24–25.

8. Genesis 1:24–25

_____

_____

_____

_____

9. Genesis 1:26–28

God announces the intent to make humankind "in our image, in our[1] likeness."[2] God makes humankind in his own image and with male and female identity. God blesses humankind with the blessing of procreation and gives them the command to populate the earth "and subdue it," to rule over all the living creatures in the sea, in the sky, and on the land.[3] As God's royal representative, humankind is being charged with the task of caring for and nurturing God's creation.

Write your own brief description of the world and reality portrayed in verses 1:29–2:1.

20

10. Genesis 1:29–2:1

_____

_____

_____

_____

11. Genesis 2:2–3

God rests from creation activities on the seventh day of creation.[1] God blesses and makes the seventh day holy, a day set apart from the ordinary days of work.

WORD STUDY NOTES #11

[1] Saying God "rested" (*shabat*) means God ceased the work of creating the heavens and the earth.

Discoveries

Let's summarize our discoveries from Genesis 1:1–2:3.

1. The earth does not remain in its original unproductive and vacant condition. God transforms it into a place with order and productivity and makes it the home of all that we see around and above us.

2. Everything God made has a space for its existence and a divinely assigned function that it is capable of carrying out.

3. Creation participates with God in creation activities.

4. God relates to creation by bestowing God's blessing upon it, which facilitates the creation's continued existence and growth.

5. God created humankind, both male and female, in God's image. Their individual and collective status as God's representatives is an important part of the order God established for creation.

6. God gave humankind the mandate to populate and be stewards of the earth and its creatures.

7. God finished work and rested on the seventh day.

WEEK 1, DAY 4

The Creation Story and the Story of God

If you have a study Bible, it may have references in a margin, a middle column, or footnotes that point to other biblical texts. You may find it helpful in understanding how the whole story of God ties together to look up some of those other scriptures from time to time. Whenever we read a biblical text, it is important to ask how the particular text we're reading relates to the rest of the Bible. The creation story, like all other stories in the Bible, has an integral place in the story of God. The creation theme is found in several places in the Bible in a variety of contexts.

As we already explored, the story of Genesis 1:1–2:3 is closely linked to the story of Genesis 2:4–25, which elaborates on God's making of the humans. In these verses, God gives instructions concerning the humans' life as God's image in the garden (fulfilling their vocation and enjoying their freedom while obeying divinely set limits). Together, these stories provide the setting for the story found in Genesis 3, which reports the failure of humankind to be God's image in the garden, causing disruption of the relationships God established for creation.

Other places in the Old Testament where a creation theme is notably present include but are not limited to Job 38–39; Isaiah 65:17–25; and Psalm 104. **In the space given below, write a short summary of how the creation theme is utilized in each passage.**

Job 38–39

_____

_____

_____

_____

Isaiah 65:17–25

_____

_____

_____

_____

Psalm 104

_____

_____

_____

_____

We also see the creation theme in the New Testament, in the context of the work of salvation God accomplished through Jesus Christ. **In the space given below, write a short summary of how the creation theme is utilized in the following passages.**

John 1:1–5

_____

_____

_____

_____

Ephesians 1:7–10

_____

23

_____

_____

_____

Colossians 1:15–20

_____

_____

_____

_____

Revelation 21:1–5

_____

_____

_____

_____

WEEK 1, DAY 5

Genesis and Our World Today

When we enter into the intriguing narrative of Genesis 1:1–2:3, the story becomes the lens through which we see ourselves, our world, and God's action in our world today.

1. What does the Genesis story of creation say to us about ourselves, our world, and God's action in our world today?

The order God established for creation remains unchanged (separation of light and darkness, day

and night, earth and sky, land and sea, etc.). The earth continues to enjoy productivity through

its vegetation, through procreative activities, and through human effort.

Following the above example, answer these questions about how we can understand ourselves, our world, and God's action in our world today.

2. What do you observe about the ways in which God blesses God's creation today?

_____

_____

_____

_____

_____

3. God created male and female in God's image. This indicates the equality of men and women in the sight of God. In what areas of our existence today is this equality maintained and promoted? Where do you see it not honored in our world?

_____

_____

_____

_____

_____

4. Humankind's task as bearers of the image of God is to care for and protect God's creation. What are some of the areas where our failure to bear God's image is clearly evident in the world?

_____

_____

_____

_____

_____

5. God's rest from God's work (Sabbath) is the basis for the command to follow the rhythm of work and rest (see Exodus 20:8–11). What is the attitude of our world about this way of life?

_____

_____

_____

_____

_____

Invitation and Response

God's Word always invites a response. Think about the way the Genesis account of creation speaks to us today. How does the story invite us to respond?

_____

_____

_____

_____

_____

_____

_____

_____

_____

When we insist on needing certain answers to our biblical questions, we miss the importance of receiving Scripture as the Word of God that God calls us to hear, and to which God invites us to respond.

GENESIS 2:4-25

This week we'll look at another story of creation in Genesis. Scholars think this story once existed independently of the first creation story. These two stories were skillfully woven by the writer of Genesis in such a way that, together, they make up the complete statement of creation faith in the Bible.

This second story gives a detailed account of God's making of the first humans. Some scholars consider it an expanded account of Genesis 1:26–27, which briefly states God's creation of humans as male and female. In the first story, the writer uses the verb "created" to describe God's activity. In the second story, "formed" is the verb used to describe God's making of the man (2:7). The imagery here is that of God fashioning the human being like a potter shapes clay into a vessel. The story also describes God's making of a garden, the placement of the man there with specific instructions, and the making of a woman to be a "helper" for the man.

The most difficult aspect of this story is in determining the meaning of the Hebrew noun 'adam, which occurs fifteen times in this short passage. Thirteen times, including 2:7, the noun occurs with the definite article (ha'adam), which means "the man" or "humankind/human beings." Only twice (vv. 5, 20) does it occur without the definite article ('adam), indicating a human being, or the proper noun Adam.

The NIV translates the occurrence of 'adam in 2:20 as Adam, as if that is the man's name. The NIV consistently translates ha'adam as "the man," except later, in 3:20 and 4:1, where it translates it as Adam. The noun appears twice without the definite article in 5:1, first as the proper noun Adam, then referring to the first human pair.

This multiple use of the noun in Hebrew makes it difficult to determine the meaning intended by the writer in this story. Its predominant use with the definite article has prompted many interpreters to see here the story of human beings. Its back-and-forth use could be an indication of the intent of the writer for this story to be the story of the first human couple as well as that of human beings as a whole.

27

WEEK 2, DAY 1

Listen to the story in Genesis 2:4–25 by reading it aloud several times until you become familiar with its verses, words, and phrases. Enjoy the experience of imagining the story in your mind, picturing each event as it unfolds.

28

WEEK 2, DAY 2
GENESIS 2:4-25

The Setting

As in the case of Genesis 1:1–2:3, Genesis places the events of this story as part of God's creation activities at the beginning of history. Thus, we are dealing with a story that serves as the initial setting for all the stories that will follow in Genesis. Because of its simple storytelling style and form, scholars think it may have been the earliest story of creation known to the ancient Israelites. However, we do not know how and when this story originated in ancient Israel. It is possible that it may have been part of Israel's oral traditions during the days of Moses in the thirteenth century BC. It is also likely that it was passed on orally from one generation to the next until it was fixed in the present written form during the exile of the Jews in Babylon. This story serves as the setting for the story of the first human sin reported in Genesis 3.

The Plot

Genesis 2 has a simple and straightforward organization, lacking most of the literary artistry found in Genesis 1. Responsible relationships seem to be the focus of this story. God made humans to live in faithful relationship with God, with the earth, with nonhuman creatures, and with others in the human community. The narrator develops this theme in nine short paragraphs following a simple storytelling style. **Below, write down next to each grouping of verses the main event or theme those verses report (follow the pattern provided for 2:4, 5–7, 8–9, 15–17, 21–22, 23, and 24–25).**

1. Genesis 2:4

An introductory statement by the writer.

2. Genesis 2:5–7

God remedied the unproductive condition of the earth with the provision of water and by making the man to work the ground.

3. Genesis 2:8–9

God placed the man in a beautiful and tree-filled garden that God had planted.

_____

_____

_____

_____

4. Genesis 2:10–14

_____

_____

_____

_____

_____

5. Genesis 2:15–17

God assigned the man a vocation and granted him permission to enjoy the garden but also placed

before him a prohibition concerning a particular tree.

_____

_____

_____

6. Genesis 2:18–20

_____

_____

_____

_____

_____

7. Genesis 2:21–22

God made the woman from the side of the man.

_____

_____

_____

_____

_____

8. Genesis 2:23

The man recognized his physical relationship to the woman.

_____

_____

_____

_____

9. Genesis 2:24–25

Two concluding statements by the writer; one emphasizes the union of a man and a woman; the

other reports the innocence of the first human couple.

_____

_____

_____

WEEK 2, DAY 3

What's Happening in the Story?

As we notice certain circumstances in the story, we will begin to see how they are similar to or different from the realities of our world. The story will become the lens through which we see the world in which we live today. In our study today, you may encounter words and/or phrases that are unfamiliar to you. Some of the particular words and translation choices for them have been explained in more detail in the **Word Study Notes**. If you are interested in even more help or detail, you can supplement this study with a Bible dictionary or other Bible study resource.

1. Genesis 2:4

The writer presents the story as "the account of the heavens and the earth."[1]

2. Genesis 2:5-7

The earth remains without vegetation because of the lack of rain and the absence of humans; to remedy this situation, God causes a mist to rise up from the earth and forms a human/man "from the dust of the ground."[1] Humans are creatures God fashioned out of earthly stuff. What makes the earthly creature a "living being," a creature with life, is the "breath of life" that God breathes into the creature's nostrils.[2] This wording implies that death is the withdrawal of God's breath. God's sharing of God's own breath of life with humans indicates humanity's intimate relation to God. The story also portrays the reality that God formed the man to be a partner with God in the development of the earth to make the earth a productive place.

Practice the above pattern to write a summary description of the world and reality that is portrayed in verses 8-9.

WORD STUDY NOTES #1

[1] Some interpreters read verse 4 as the conclusion of the previous story; others consider the first part of verse 4 to be the conclusion of the first story and the second part to be the opening of the next story. It is appropriate to read verse 4 as both the conclusion of the previous story and the opening of the second story.

WORD STUDY NOTES #2

[1] The word translated "man" here (ha'adam) means literally the man, or humans. The word translated "ground" is 'adamah in Hebrew. The wordplay ('adam from 'adamah) indicates humanity's intimate relation to the ground.

[2] "Living being" (nephesh hayah) is also the term used for animals in Genesis 1:20, 24. God's breathing of God's own life-giving breath into the nostrils of the human is what distinguishes humans from animals. This act is, perhaps, what constitutes humans as created in the image of God.

3. Genesis 2:8–9[1, 2, 3]

_____

_____

_____

_____

4. Genesis 2:10–14

These verses portray the garden as a well-watered and life-sustaining place near a river that flows from Eden. From the Eden area, the river branches off into four tributaries that meander through a large geographical area. These verses portray the reality of the river that flows from Eden as the source of the wealth, beauty, and productivity of not only the garden but also of the world outside the garden.

Create your own brief description of the world/reality portrayed in verses 15–17.

5. Genesis 2:15-17

_____

_____

_____

_____

6. Genesis 2:18–20

God observed the aloneness of the man and decided to remedy the situation.[1] These verses portray the wild animals and birds as living creatures that God formed out of the ground. Though the man established relationship with the animals by naming them but did not find among them a suitable helper for him.[2] It is important to note that, although both humans and animals are living creatures, there is no mention of God breathing God's own breath of life into the nostrils of animals, like God is shown to have done for humanity in verse 7.

WORD STUDY NOTES #3

[1] "Eden" in this story is a geographical region in the east—meaning east of the land of Israel. The garden itself is not called Eden, as we often assume; rather, the garden is located _in_ a larger region or place called Eden.

[2] The "tree of life" perhaps refers to the possibility of living forever (see 3:22). Verse 16 implies that the man is free to eat from this tree.

[3] Commentators give various explanations for "the tree of the knowledge of good and evil." This tree perhaps indicates the limit of human freedom in the garden.

WORD STUDY NOTES #6

[1] "It is not good" is the opposite of the repeated evaluation "it was good" in the first creation story.

[2] "Helper" (_'ezer_) occurs only twenty-one times in the Hebrew Bible. Eight times the noun refers to God's help. Eleven times the noun means "strength" or "power." These references clearly indicate that the word we have translated as "helper" from verses 18 and 20 does not mean a subordinate person; instead, it means a source of strength and support.

WORD STUDY NOTES #7

[1] God causes a "deep sleep," perhaps to prevent the man from seeing God in action (see Genesis 15:12–17). The Israelites believed that no one could see God and yet live (see Exodus 33:19-23).

WORD STUDY NOTES #8

[1] The similar-sounding Hebrew words for "woman" (*'isha*) and "man" (*'ish*) convey the man's recognition of the woman's relationship and likeness to him.

WORD STUDY NOTES #9

[1] These verses are the observations and comments of the writer of Genesis.

[2] "That is why" refers to the physical likeness and sexual distinction that the man discovers in the woman.

[3] "Naked" here may refer to a state of childlike innocence, or it may be an image of transparency and integrity in relationships. Either way, humans did not experience shame in their relationship to each other.

Write your own brief description of the world and reality portrayed in verses 21–22.

7. Genesis 2:21–22[1]

_____

_____

_____

_____

_____

8. Genesis 2:23

The man recognizes the woman's physical relationship and likeness to him and names her "woman."[1]

9. Genesis 2:24–25[1]

Verse 24 portrays the establishment of a new family unit by the social and sexual union of a man and woman in marriage.[2] Verse 25 portrays the reality of innocence and transparency that characterized the relationships (both between the man and the woman *and* between the humans and God) in the garden.[3]

Discoveries

Let's summarize our discoveries from Genesis 2:4–25.

1. The earth's productivity depends on the collaborative efforts of God and human beings.

2. Human beings are earthly creatures formed by God, and they depend on God for their vitality.

3. God assigned the first humans the task of cultivating the garden and gave them the freedom to enjoy the garden.

4. God set a limit to the first humans' freedom and warned them of death as the consequence of their disobedience.

5. Solitude is not God's plan for human existence.

6. The human task includes the establishment of proper relationship with the animal world.

7. Both men and women are formed by God, and they are physically related to each other; they are God's gift to each other for intimacy and relationships.

8. Humans began their history with innocence and transparency in relationships.

WEEK 2, DAY 4

The Creation Story and the Story of God

Let's consider some of the biblical passages that show the relationship of Genesis 2:4–25 to the larger story of God in the Bible. To begin with, this story is the setting of the story told in Genesis 3. A proper understanding of Genesis 2 is important for a proper understanding of Genesis 3. **In the space given below, write a short summary of how the story of Genesis 2:4–25 is reflected in the each passage.**

Psalm 65:9–10

_____

_____

_____

_____

_____

_____

Genesis 3:19; Job 4:19; Psalm 90:3; Isaiah 64:8

_____

_____

_____

_____

_____

_____

1 Corinthians 15:45–49

_____

_____

_____

_____

_____

_____

Isaiah 51:3; Ezekiel 28:13; 31:8–9; Joel 2:3

_____
_____
_____
_____
_____
_____

Psalm 46:4; Isaiah 33:21; Ezekiel 47:1–12; Revelation 22:1–2

_____
_____
_____
_____
_____
_____

Proverbs 11:30; 13:12; 15:4; Revelation 2:7; 22:2

_____
_____
_____
_____
_____
_____

Matthew 19:5; Mark 10:7–8; 1 Corinthians 6:16; Ephesians 5:31

_____
_____
_____
_____
_____

WEEK 2, DAY 5

Genesis and Our World Today

When we enter into this fascinating narrative of Genesis 2:4–25, the story becomes the lens through which we see ourselves, our world, and God's action in our world today.

1. What does this Genesis story say to us about ourselves, our world, and God's action in our world today?

Our secular world often views the productivity of the earth solely as the result of humans' hard work and the use of proper resources; our story reminds us that it is the outcome of the combined efforts of God and humans. We often forget the fact that we are made of materials that can be easily broken down and that our strength and vitality depend on the breath of life that comes from God.

Following the above example, answer these questions about how we can understand ourselves, our world, and God's action in our world today.

2. Though the story focuses on cultivating the garden as the human vocation, work involves a variety of areas and professions today. How often do we view our work as a partnership with God? What is the general attitude toward work in our world?

_____

_____

_____

_____

_____

3. What are some of the freedoms that you enjoy today? How do you respond to freedoms that come with a limit? What are some of the consequences we see in the world today of people whose actions are based on their claim of absolute freedom? Give examples.

_____

_____

_____

_____

_____

4. Though God's desire for humans is not to experience solitude, loneliness is a reality for many people today. Why are there so many lonely people in our world? How do we contribute to the loneliness of others?

_____

_____

_____

_____

_____

5. What is our attitude toward animals that are not our house pets? How do we treat them?

_____

_____

_____

_____

_____

6. What value do we give to truth-telling, transparency, and integrity in our relationships? Cite some examples of areas where these values are lacking in our world.

_____

_____

_____

_____

_____

Invitation and Response

God's Word always invites a response. Think about the way the second account of creation in Genesis speaks to us today. How does the story invite us to respond?

_____

_____

_____

_____

40

We often forget that we are made of materials that can be easily broken down and that our strength and vitality depend on the breath of life that comes from God.

GENESIS 3

Genesis 3 is commonly known as the story of the fall. The Christian doctrine of original sin has its foundation in this story. Many Christians see in this story the explanation of how evil came into the world. Many Christians also identify the serpent in this story as Satan, who — in popular thinking — was a fallen angel.

However, it is important for us to begin our study with the awareness that the Hebrew words for "sin," "evil," "Satan," and "the devil" do not occur in this story. Whatever connections we make between the serpent and Satan do not derive from the story itself. They are speculations deriving from other biblical passages (see Ezekiel 28:11–19; Revelation 12:7–12; 20:2).

These popular beliefs continue to shape the way we hear this story today. Although it is not easy to set aside popular beliefs, we should make every attempt to listen to the text during this study as if we are hearing it for the first time.

WEEK 3, DAY 1

Listen to the story in Genesis 3 by reading it aloud several times until you become familiar with its verses, words, and phrases. Enjoy the experience of imagining the story in your mind, picturing each event as it unfolds.

WEEK 3, DAY 2
GENESIS 3

The Setting

The reference to the serpent as one of the wild animals God made (v. 1) links this story to the creation stories (see 1:24–25; 2:19–20). Obviously this creature is part of the animal world that God has placed under the authority of humankind, the image of God (see 1:28).

The second creation story (2:4–25) provides the immediate setting of Genesis 3. It assumes the garden as the home of the first human pair. The man has already exercised authority over the animals by naming them (2:19–20). The serpent is included in the world of animals that the man has named. The story in chapter 3 anticipates the first human couple's continued exercise of their authority as the image of God in the garden.

The story also focuses on the issue of human freedom, a key theme in the previous story (2:16–17). The theme of human nakedness is another link between the two stories (see 2:25; 3:7). The story is also verbally connected to the previous story by the similar-sounding words *'arummim* ("naked" in 2:25) and *'arum* ("crafty" in 3:1).

This story ends with the expulsion of the first human pair from the garden; the events of chapter 4 take place outside the garden.

The Plot

Genesis 3 is like a crime drama with four major scenes: the violation, the trial, the verdict, and the punishment. These scenes focus on how the garden became a place of disrupted relationships. For the purpose of our study, we divide this story into eight paragraphs to examine. Below, write down next to each grouping of verses the main event or theme those verses report (follow the pattern provided for 3:1–5, 6–7, 14–15, and 17–19).

1. Genesis 3:1–5

A conversation occurs between the serpent and the woman about the consequence of eating the

forbidden fruit.

_____

_____

_____

2. Genesis 3:6–7

The humans eat the fruit, recognize their nakedness, and attempt to conceal it.

3. Genesis 3:8–13

4. Genesis 3:14–15

God sentences the serpent.

5. Genesis 3:16

6. Genesis 3:17–19

God sentences the man.

7. Genesis 3:20

_____

_____

_____

_____

_____

8. Genesis 3:21–24

_____

_____

_____

_____

_____

WEEK 3, DAY 3

What's Happening in the Story?

As we notice certain circumstances in the story, we will begin to see how they are similar to or different from the realities of our world. The story will become the lens through which we see the world in which we live today. In our study today, you may encounter words and/or phrases that are unfamiliar to you. Some of the particular words and translation choices for them have been explained in more detail in the **Word Study Notes**. If you are interested in even more help or detail, you can supplement this study with a Bible dictionary or other Bible study resource.

WORD STUDY NOTES #1

[1] The Hebrew word *'arum* ("cunning, crafty, shrewd," etc.) sounds similar to *'arummim* ("naked"). The story, through a play on words, shows that the first human couple's yielding to the voice of a cunning (*'arum*) creature resulted in their knowledge of their nakedness (*'arummim*).

[2] Though the conversation appears to happen exclusively between the serpent and the woman, verse 6 indicates that the man is a present and willing participant during the entire conversation ("her husband, who was with her").

1. Genesis 3:1-5

The story begins with the portrayal of the serpent as the craftiest[1] of all the animals God made. The serpent initiates a conversation with the woman[2] by asking a misleading question implying that God's prohibition included all the trees in the garden. The woman responds with a correction, but she makes the prohibition more severe by stating that not only eating the fruit but also merely *touching* it would result in their death. The serpent asserts that the humans will not die. The serpent also claims that God knows the potential benefits of the forbidden fruit. By eating the fruit, the humans will become like God, knowing good and evil.

2. Genesis 3:6-7

The conversation with the serpent ends without any actual coercion from the serpent. The woman does not respond to the serpent but simply reflects on the potential benefits the tree offers. She sees its similarity to all other trees in two ways: it offers food, and it is beautiful. In addition, she sees the tree's potential as a source of wisdom. The woman and the man choose to eat the forbidden fruit after all. As the serpent promised, the humans' eyes are then opened. They see their nakedness — which is not a matter of shame in a trusting and transparent relationship with God and each other — as something that needs to be covered. So they attempt to conceal their nakedness from God and from each other by making garments out of leaves.

Practice the above pattern to write a summary description of the realities portrayed in the next few verses.

3. Genesis 3:8–13

_____

_____

_____

_____

_____

_____

4. Genesis 3:14–15

Following the trial of the humans, God acts as judge and pronounces a sentence on each of the parties involved in the violation of the command. God does not question the serpent because the woman already implicated the serpent in her response to God. God pronounces the judgment as a curse on the serpent that effectively excludes the serpent from the rest of the animals. God also decrees for the serpent a life of humiliation, relegating it to a crawling and dust-eating way of life. God also decrees for the serpent and the human race a relationship of enmity that will begin with the woman and the serpent and continue between the offspring of both. God thus implements a change in the relationship between humans and the serpent. God's decree announces that this ongoing conflict will lead to the crushing of the serpent's head by the woman's offspring and the striking of the heel of the latter by the former.[1]

5. Genesis 3:16

God's sentence on the woman is not a curse but merely the consequence of her action. Pregnancy and delivery of children will become difficult and painful for the woman. The woman, however, will continue to desire sexual intimacy with her husband. She will also be ruled by her husband. Their shared disobedience of God thus results in the disruption of the relationship God established for them.

WORD STUDY NOTES #4

[1] Verses 14–15 have been generally interpreted in two ways over the centuries. Some see here an explanation of why snakes crawl on their bellies and why human beings' immediate reaction when they encounter snakes is to kill them by crushing their heads. The Jewish and Christian traditions have interpreted these verses as a messianic text that predicts God's ultimate victory over the deceiver (Satan) through the seed of the woman (the Messiah). We do not need to give preference to one and exclude the other from our hearing of this story.

6. Genesis 3:17–19[1]

_____

_____

_____

_____

_____

_____

7. Genesis 3:20

Adam, by naming his wife Eve,[1] expresses his confidence that life will continue, despite God's verdict of death because of their sin.

8. Genesis 3:21–24[1, 2]

_____

_____

_____

_____

_____

_____

Discoveries

Let's summarize our discoveries from Genesis 3.

1. The serpent, the seducer, was a creature made by God.

2. By asking a deceitful question, the serpent claimed that the humans' freedom in the garden was severely restricted by God.

3. By exaggerating God's command, the woman acknowledged the humans' fear of death caused by God's prohibition.

4. The serpent implied that God was untrustworthy and asserted itself as a truth-teller by its claim that God had withheld from the humans God's knowledge about the tree.

5. The humans' act of disobedience resulted in shame and loss of innocence, which they attempted to cover up by their own scheme.

6. God's questions were aimed to seek the humans' confession of their disobedience.

7. The humans blamed someone else for their action (God, the woman, the serpent)—a clear sign of the breaking of relationships.

8. God's curse of the ground indicates that the humans' sin resulted in the breaking of their relationship to the ground.

9. God announced the return of humans, taken from dust, to dust.

10. By clothing the humans, God extended grace to those have estranged themselves from God.

11. God expelled the sinners from God's presence and eliminated the possibility of humans ever attaining immortality by their own efforts.

12. Banishment from the garden did not mean the end of the humans' partnership with God in the development of creation through their vocation.

WEEK 3, DAY 4

The Story of the Fall and the Story of God

Let's now consider some of the biblical passages that show the relationship of Genesis 3 to the larger story of God in the Bible. The Old Testament itself does not directly refer to this story, though scholars see some parallel between this story and Ezekiel's lament over the king of Tyre in Ezekiel 28:11–19. Ezekiel compares the fall of the king to the expulsion of a "guardian cherub" from the mount of God to the earth. It is possible that this story may have inspired the prophet to compose the language of the lament over the fallen king of Tyre.

The events reported in Genesis 4 take place outside the garden. Adam and Eve are mentioned there only in connection with the birth of their two sons. They are mentioned again in the report of the birth of their third son, Seth, at the end of chapter 4. The genealogy of Adam in chapter 5 reports that Adam died at the age of 930 years (vv. 1–5).

The apocryphal book The Wisdom of Solomon links the entrance of death into the world to the devil (2:24). However, another apocryphal book connects death specifically to the woman (Sirach 25:24).

Listed below are several passages from the Bible that show some relationship to the story of Genesis 3, whether directly or indirectly. **In the space given below, write a short summary of how the theme of the fall (or any other theme you notice from Genesis 3) is utilized or referenced in each passage.**

Psalm 90:3; Psalm 104:29; Ecclesiastes 12:7

_____

_____

_____

_____

_____

_____

Proverbs 1:7

_____

_____

_____

_____

_____

_____

Matthew 4:1–11

_____

_____

_____

_____

_____

_____

Romans 5:12–21; 2 Corinthians 5:17–21

_____

_____

_____

_____

_____

_____

Romans 16:20

_____

_____

_____

_____

_____

_____

2 Corinthians 11:3

_____

_____

_____

_____

_____

_____

Revelation 22:2

_____

_____

_____

_____

_____

_____

WEEK 3, DAY 5

Genesis and Our World Today

When we enter into this fascinating narrative of Genesis 3, the story becomes the lens through which we can see ourselves, our world, and God's action in our world today.

1. What does the Genesis story of the fall say to us about ourselves, our world, and God's action in our world today?

Deception is a reality in our world. We live in a world where anything and anyone within God's

creation can attempt to seduce us away from God.

_____

_____

_____

_____

_____

Following the above example, answer these questions about how we can understand ourselves, our world, and God's action in our world today.

2. What are some of the distortions and misrepresentations of God's Word you have encountered in your life?

_____

_____

_____

_____

_____

3. Why do we often trust the voices we hear in our world over the voice of God?

_____

_____

_____

_____

_____

4. What are some of the negative outcomes of blaming others for our actions?

_____

_____

_____

_____

_____

5. What are some of the negative effects of male domination of women in our world today?

_____

_____

_____

_____

_____

6. What hope do you find for us sinners in God's provision of clothing for the first human couple?

_____

_____

_____

_____

_____

7. What hope do you find in the rest of the biblical story for the sinful humans' restored relationship with God?

_____

_____

_____

_____

_____

Invitation and Response

God's Word always invites a response. Think about the way the Genesis account of the fall speaks to us today. How does the story invite us to respond?

_____

_____

_____

_____

_____

_____

_____

_____

_____

_____

_____

_____

_____

_____

_____

55

_____

_____

_____

_____

_____

_____

_____

_____

_____

_____

_____

_____

_____

_____

Banishment from the garden did not mean the end of the humans' partnership with God in the development of creation through their vocation.

GENESIS 4:1-16

This story introduces us to the realities of life outside the garden of Eden. Adam and Eve remain in the background as the first parents, and do not play any active role in the story. The story focuses on their two sons, their worship of God, and the murder of the younger son by his older brother. The story indicates that the two brothers are involved in different vocations — one in farming and one in shepherding. Farmers and shepherds were the two earliest socioeconomic groups in human history.

This story also records the first known instance of worship in the Bible. The story does not say how the brothers learned of the need to worship or if there was an established pattern of worship. The story implies that their worship was motivated by their desire to find favor with God.

Some scholars have suggested that this story explains the long history of conflict between farmers (settlers) and shepherds (nomads) in the ancient world. Some others have interpreted the story as Israel's explanation for the nomadic life of the Kenites (presumably the descendants of Cain), who lived on the edge of the desert south of the land of Canaan. These views are based on speculation and do not add much to our understanding of the story. As we find it in the Bible, this story shows the continuation of human rebellion against God outside the garden. It manifests itself in a violent act, leading to further breakdown of relationship between God and humankind.

The story of Cain and Abel is the first of a number of stories in the Bible in which a brother-brother relationship receives attention. Some of the most well-known are: Esau and Jacob (Genesis 27), Joseph and his brothers (Genesis 37), Amnon and Absalom (2 Samuel 13), Solomon and Adonijah (1 Kings 2), and the two brothers in Jesus's parable of the prodigal son (Luke 15).

WEEK 4, DAY 1

Listen to the story in Genesis 4:1–16 by reading it aloud several times until you become familiar with its verses, words, and phrases. Enjoy the experience of imagining the story in your mind, picturing each event as it unfolds.

WEEK 4, DAY 2
GENESIS 4:1–16

The Setting

The introduction of Adam and his wife in verse 1 makes clear that this story is a continuation of the preceding story of the first humans' rebellion and their expulsion from the garden. The story takes place outside the garden; the first human couple live without access to the tree of life. By rebelling against God, they have claimed equality with God. They have become, in their presumptuous thinking, Godlike in knowledge, freedom, and decision-making.

The setting of this story also includes the disrupted relationships that resulted from the first sin. Cain and Abel may have brought their offerings in an attempt to restore their relationship with God and to find their way back into the garden.

The story continues with Cain as the surviving son of the first parents (vv. 17–24). At this point, the story presupposes other human beings in the world. Cain finds a wife and becomes a city builder. Cain's history disappears from the Bible after the fifth generation of his descendants. Humankind's history is continued in the Bible through the line of Seth, the third son born to Adam and Eve (4:25ff.).

The Plot

This story, like Genesis 3 before it, is structured like a crime drama, with five major scenes: the birth of Cain and Abel, offerings made by Cain and Abel, God's speech to Cain, Cain's crime, and the trial and verdict. These scenes focus on human sin intensifying the already disrupted relationships in God's creation. **Below, write down next to each grouping of verses the main event or theme those verses report (follow the pattern provided for vv. 1–2, 3–5, and 9–16).**

1: Genesis 4:1–2
Adam and his wife became parents of two sons, Cain and Abel.

_____

_____

_____

_____

_____

_____

2. Genesis 4:3-5

Both Cain and Abel brought offerings to God, but Cain became upset because of God's negative response to his offering.

_____

_____

_____

_____

3. Genesis 4:6-7

_____

_____

_____

_____

_____

_____

4. Genesis 4:8

_____

_____

_____

_____

_____

_____

5: Genesis 4:9-16

God confronted Cain, but he refused to admit his guilt; God sentenced Cain to a life of wandering the earth.

_____

_____

_____

_____

WEEK 4, DAY 3

What's Happening in the Story?

As we notice certain circumstances in the story, we will begin to see how they are similar to or different from the realities of our world. The story will become the lens through which we see the world in which we live today. In our study today, you may encounter words and/or phrases that are unfamiliar to you. Some of the particular words and translation choices for them have been explained in more detail in the **Word Study Notes**. If you are interested in even more help or detail, you can supplement this study with a Bible dictionary or other Bible study resource.

1. Genesis 4:1–2

Even though Adam and Eve have been expelled from the garden, they fulfill the creation mandate to "be fruitful and increase in number" (Genesis 1:28). The story begins with the report of the sexual activity[1] between Adam and Eve, and Eve's pregnancy and childbirth. Eve acknowledges God's activity in her life that makes it possible for her to give birth to a male child. The narrator presents Abel as "his brother," not as Eve's son. A focus on the brother-brother relationship was perhaps an agenda of the writer of this story. Cain follows the vocation that was assigned to Adam, to be a tiller of the ground (see 2:15; 3:23). Abel chooses a vocation as a shepherd. We may see here an allusion to humankind's vocation as caretakers of the animal world in Genesis 1:28. We do not know why the story gives preference to Abel's vocation by mentioning it first.

2. Genesis 4:3–5

These verses portray the scene of the first acts of worship recorded in the Bible. Without giving any details, the story reports the offerings brought by the brothers. Based on God's response and Cain's reaction, we assume that the brothers are seeking God's favor. Cain, the tiller of the ground, brings a produce offering, the work of his hands. Abel, the keeper of flocks, also brings the yield of his labor, the firstborn of his animals. We do not know why the LORD regards only Abel's offering with favor, nor are we told how Cain discovers God's rejection of his offering.[1] Cain reacts to God's response with expressions of dejection and distress.[2]

3. Genesis 4:6–7

Though God does not regard Cain or his offering with favor, God does speak to him. God's speech begins with two rhetorical questions, the answers to which are obvious. These questions do not convey the tone of accusation or God's indictment of Cain. God asks these questions to engage Cain, who is depressed. God's questions imply God's concern for Cain's emotional well-being.[1] By asking questions, God is also letting Cain know that God's rejection of Cain's offering does not mean an end to God's relationship with Cain. God's questions also imply that Cain's positive response to God will put Cain on the path toward right relationship with God. God's speech ends with an instruction and a warning. If Cain keeps a proper attitude about God's response to their offerings, his relationship with God will be restored. His face will be lifted up because he will find favor with God.[2] God also warns that if Cain remains depressed about God's response to his offering, then Cain will become a victim of the power of sin.[3] God uses the image of a powerful and predatory animal waiting nearby to ambush its prey to portray the reality of the power of sin. God counsels Cain that, though the desire of the power of sin is to gain entrance into his life and destroy him, Cain should not let that happen. Instead, Cain must exercise his power over sin and master it.[4] Otherwise it will destroy his life.

Practice the above pattern to write a summary description of the world and reality that is portrayed in verse 8.

4. Genesis 4:8[1, 2]

_____

_____

_____

_____

_____

5. Genesis 4:9–10[1,2]

_____

_____

_____

_____

_____

6. Genesis 4:11–12[1,2]

_____

_____

_____

_____

_____

_____

7. Genesis 4:13–14[1]

_____

_____

_____

_____

_____

_____

8. Genesis 4:15–16[1]

_____

_____

_____

_____

_____

63

WORD STUDY NOTES #5

[1] God's question to Cain is very similar to God's question of "Where are you?" to the man in Genesis 3:9.

[2] Cain's question "Am I my brother's keeper?" seems to imply that God, not Cain, is responsible for Abel's well-being.

WORD STUDY NOTES #6

[1] Blood is the seat of life, according to the Israelite beliefs (see Leviticus 17:11). Genesis 9:5–6 describes the value God places on the blood/life of humans. God created humans in God's image; God's life-breath is in them (Genesis 2:7). Thus, human life belongs to God; killing is prohibited because it is a violation of God's property rights over human life (see Exodus 20:13).

[2] The bond between humans and the ground is made clear in Genesis 2:7, 15; 3:23. Cain, a tiller of the ground, has broken his relationship with the ground by forcing it to receive his brother's spilled blood.

WORD STUDY NOTES #7

[1] Cain's fear of retribution implies the existence of other human beings.

WORD STUDY NOTES #8

[1] We do not know what the mark on Cain looked like or where it was placed. The Hebrew phrase could also be translated as "appointed a sign for Cain" (see NASB).

Discoveries

Let's summarize our discoveries from Genesis 4:1–16.

1. Normal life activities continue outside the garden, though the first humans' sin damages their relationship with God.

2. The first humans fulfill the creation mandate to be involved in procreation.

3. Both Cain and Abel bring offerings to God from their respective vocations. Abel and his offering receive God's favor, but Cain and his offering do not.

4. Cain is depressed because of God's rejection of his offering. God graciously engages Cain even though God rejected Cain's offering.

5. God instructs Cain to keep a proper attitude about God's response to the offerings of the brothers. God counsels Cain that Cain will be accepted if he obeys God's instruction.

6. God warns Cain about the power of sin waiting to ambush him like a predatory animal. God invites Cain to master the power of sin before it makes inroads into his life.

7. Cain rejects God's instruction and warning, murders his brother, and then denies any responsibility for Abel's well-being.

8. Cain's violence results in the breaking of his relationship with the ground.

9. God condemns Cain to a life of restless wandering on the earth.

10. Cain complains about the severity of his punishment, so God announces God's judgment on anyone who would take Cain's life and places him under God's protective care.

11. Cain leaves the presence of God and lives his life as a wanderer.

WEEK 4, DAY 4

The Cain-Abel Story and the Story of God

Let's now consider some of the biblical passages that show the relationship of Genesis 4:1–16 to the larger story of God in the Bible. Cain's story ends in chapter 4, and he disappears from the Bible entirely. His name appears again only in Numbers 24:22 (the NIV translation "Kenites" is Cain in the Hebrew text); the name suggests the ancestry of the Kenites. When Eve gives birth to Seth, she acknowledges him as God's replacement for Abel. Though Cain and Abel are not mentioned again in the Old Testament, we find a few references to them in the New Testament. **In the space given below, write a short summary of how each passage might relate to the Cain and Abel story.**

Psalm 133

_____

_____

_____

_____

_____

Matthew 5:21–24

_____

_____

_____

_____

_____

Matthew 23:35; Luke 11:50–51

_____

_____

_____

_____

_____

Hebrews 11:4

_____

_____

_____

_____

_____

_____

Hebrews 12:24

_____

_____

_____

_____

_____

_____

1 John 2:9–11

_____

_____

_____

_____

_____

_____

1 John 3:12

_____

_____

_____

_____

_____

_____

Jude 11

_____

_____

_____

_____

_____

_____

67

WEEK 4, DAY 5

Genesis and Our World Today

When we enter into this fascinating narrative of Genesis 4, the story becomes the lens through which we see ourselves, our world, and God's action in our world today.

1. What does the Genesis story of Cain and Abel say to us about ourselves, our world, and God's action in our world today?

God's creational purposes continue to be at work in our sinful world through human propagation and population growth.

Though we may not be fully aware of it, through our vocational choices we fulfill God's creational intent for us to be engaged in work for the well-being of creation.

The strong among us (Cain) often fail to care for and sustain the weak and the powerless (Abel) in the world.

We live in a world in which different perspectives and attitudes toward worship have often become divisive issues among the people of God.

Our negative attitude toward God is often the result of our misperception of God's lack of concern for us (such as an unanswered prayer).

We often disregard God's instructions about proper relationships and the warnings about sin that we hear in the setting of worship.

Though we are able to resist the power of sin, we let it reign over us.

The breakup of stable and healthy relationships due to the hurtful actions of people is an everyday reality in our world.

Following the above example, answer these questions about how we can understand ourselves, our world, and God's action in our world today.

2. How do we respond when God speaks to us about our wrong attitudes and wrongful actions?

_____

_____

_____

3. In what areas of our existence today do we hear echoes of Cain's question, "Am I my brother's keeper?"

_____

_____

_____

_____

_____

_____

4. Cain did not show any mercy to his brother, but he thought his punishment from God was too severe. Why do people in our day expect grace (from God and others) that they are not willing to give to others?

_____

_____

_____

_____

_____

_____

Invitation and Response

God's Word always invites a response. Think about the way the Genesis account of Cain and Abel speaks to us today. How does the story invite us to respond?

_____

_____

_____

_____

_____

_____

_____

_____

Our negative attitude toward God is often the result of our misperception of God's lack of concern for us (such as unanswered prayer).

GENESIS 6:5-22

The story of a few people escaping a catastrophic flood in a boat by heeding the warnings and instructions of gods is part of the memory and narrative tradition of numerous ancient cultures.

The most widely known is the story of Utnapishtim in the *Epic of Gilgamesh*, from ancient Mesopotamia. There are a number of similarities between the story of Noah and that of Utnapishtim. The most striking similarities include the following: the flood in both stories was divinely ordained; both Noah and Utnapishtim heeded the deity's warning and escaped the flood in a vessel they built according to divine instructions; both men sent out a dove and a raven after their vessels grounded on a mountain; both men offered sacrifices after leaving the vessel. There are some differences in the details, including the number of people in the boat and, in Utnapishtim's case, the gods' granting of his immortality.

Stories like that of Utnapishtim show that the biblical story of the flood is not fictional; rather, it is part of Israel's collective memory of the story of humanity. In the biblical account, we find the Israelite belief that the flood, the escape of Noah and his family, and God's covenant with Noah and his family were all actions taken by God to provide a new beginning for humanity.

Since both stories are set in the Mesopotamian region, scholars believe that these stories relate to a major flood in the Tigris-Euphrates river valley. This region was the earliest-known world in the ancient times and the seat of the first-known human civilization.

The flood story in Genesis begins in 6:5 and doesn't end until 9:17. The focus of this study is 6:5–22, where we find God's indictment of humankind and the instructions God gives to Noah to prepare for the flood.

WEEK 5, DAY 1

Listen to the story in Genesis 6:5–22 by reading it aloud several times until you become familiar with its verses, words, and phrases. Enjoy the experience of imagining the story in your mind, picturing each event as it unfolds.

The Setting

We have been following the story of God that begins in the Bible with the story of creation (Genesis 1–2). We saw in Genesis 3 how humans, whom God created in God's image, disobeyed God's command, thus disrupting their relationships with God, others, and the rest of creation. The story of Cain showed how violence became part of the story of humankind (Genesis 4). As humans increased and multiplied, violence and wickedness also increased on the earth (Genesis 5:1–6:5). In the genealogy of Adam, Enoch is the only one who walked faithfully with God (5:21–24). The story of the marriage of "the sons of God" and "the daughters of humans" (6:1–4) implies that sin became cosmic in scope, breaking down the boundary between heaven and earth. Though the details of this story pose unanswerable questions, we can safely assume that violence and aggressive behavior increased with the appearance of the Nephilim (literally, "the fallen ones") on the earth (6:4).

This continued growth of violence and wickedness on the earth is the setting in which we find the beginning of the story of Noah in Genesis 6:5–22. Noah is introduced in our story as someone who walked faithfully with God, thus following the example set forth by Enoch.

The flood story itself is the focus of chapter 7. Noah's actions after the floodwaters receded and dried up from the earth are reported in chapter 8. The beginning of a new humanity through Noah and his family, and God's covenant with them and the whole creation, bring the flood story to its proper conclusion in Genesis 9.

The Plot

Let's now look at how the writer organizes the beginning section of the flood story.

We will divide the story into seven paragraphs to examine. **Write down next to each grouping of verses the main event theme those verses report (follow the pattern provided for 6:5–8, 9–10, 11–13, and 17–18).**

1. Genesis 6:5–8
These verses provide the rationale for God's decision to wipe out the human race.

2. Genesis 6:9–10
These verses describe Noah's relationship with God and give the names of his three sons.

3. Genesis 6:11–13

These verses repeat the rationale for God's decision to destroy all humans and the earth.

_____

4. Genesis 6:14–16

_____

_____

_____

_____

_____

5. Genesis 6:17–18

God offers a future relationship with Noah even though God has determined to destroy the earth

with floodwaters.

_____

6. Genesis 6:19–21

_____

_____

_____

_____

_____

7. Genesis 6:22

_____

_____

_____

_____

_____

WEEK 5, DAY 3

What's Happening in the Story?

As we notice certain circumstances in the story, we will begin to see how they are similar to or different from the realities of our world. The story will become the lens through which we see the world in which we live today. In our study today, you may encounter words and/or phrases that are unfamiliar to you. Some of the particular words and translation choices for them have been explained in more detail in the **Word Study Notes**. If you are interested in even more help or detail, you can supplement this study with a Bible dictionary or other Bible study resource.

WORD STUDY NOTES #1

[1] In Hebrew thought, the heart (*leb*) represents the inner being; it is where human will, emotions, thinking, and planning originate.

[2] The verb "wipe" means to erase, blot out, wash, etc. This verb conveys the image of flooding as the means of God's judgment that will result in the cleansing, or washing, of the wickedness of the human race.

1. Genesis 6:5–8

The writer reports God's evaluation of the human race. God's indictment of the human race is not based on one particular act of wickedness that God happens to observe. God looks into the human condition since the catastrophe in the garden and sees that wickedness has increased on the earth as the humans have multiplied. What God once saw as "good" has become corrupt and wicked. God's assessment of humans also includes the condition of their hearts; God sees that every thought that originates in the heart is evil.[1] In verse 6, the writer presents the response of God's heart to the total corruption of the human heart. God "regrets" that God created and placed humans on the earth. Moreover, human wickedness has placed a deep and painful tension within God's heart. God is described as "deeply troubled" about the joyful creation that has turned away from God.

Verse 7 reports that God decided to undo what God created—both humans and animals ("wipe from the face of the earth").[2] God's change of mind about creating the human race leads to God's decision to return the earth to its condition when there was no life. God's granting of God's "favor" to Noah (v. 8) signals hope for the future of the human race. God extends grace to a human being in the midst of God's painful decision to undo creation.

Practice the above pattern to write a summary description of the world and reality that is portrayed in verses 9–10.

2. Genesis 6:9-10[1, 2, 3]

_____

_____

_____

_____

_____

3. Genesis 6:11-13[1, 2]

_____

_____

_____

_____

_____

4. Genesis 6:14-16

God gave Noah instructions to build a spacious ark and water-proof it inside and out.[1] The dimensions (450 feet long, 75 feet wide, 45 feet high) and the roof indicate that it is essentially supposed to be a floating house. Instructions also include the making of a door on the side and three decks in the interior of the ark. Some scholars think that the opening of one cubit (18 inches) all around, below the roof, would have provided ventilation.

5. Genesis 6:17-18

In verse 17, God specifically mentions "floodwaters" as the means by which God will destroy all life on the earth.[1] The covenant God promises to establish with Noah in verse 18 perhaps means God's commitment to protect Noah and his family from the floodwaters that will destroy everything on earth. They are to enter the ark in order to experience the reality of God's promise of presence and protection.

77

WORD STUDY NOTES #2

[1] The word "righteous" (*tsaddiq*) indicates Noah's right relationship with God and others in his world.

[2] "Blameless" (*tamim*) does not mean that Noah is sinless but that he is a person of high integrity.

[3] "Walked faithfully with God" indicates a way of life that demonstrates close relationship with God.

WORD STUDY NOTES #3

[1] The word "corrupt" (*shahat*) indicates a ruined or decayed condition. The verb translated "destroy" in verse 17 comes from the same verb. God's judgment of destruction completes the ruin that humans have already started.

[2] "Violence" (*hamas*) refers to lawless acts and a willful disregard for the moral order, which often results in murderous deeds.

WORD STUDY NOTES #4

[1] The word "ark" (*tebah*) is the same word used in Exodus to describe the basket made by Moses's mother to save her infant son.

WORD STUDY NOTES #5

[1] The word translated "floodwaters" (*mabbul*) probably refers to the waters above the sky in Genesis 1:7.

Write your own brief description of the world/reality portrayed in verses 19–21 and verse 22.

6. Genesis 6:19–21

_____

_____

_____

_____

_____

7. Genesis 6:22

_____

_____

_____

_____

_____

Discoveries

Let's summarize our discoveries from Genesis 6:5–22.

1. God's continued care for God's creation includes God's careful and ongoing assessment of the conduct of creation.

2. By the time Noah enters the story of God, humans have become thoroughly wicked, not only in their actions but also in their inner being.

3. In grief and agony, God decides to undo God's creation that is already on the path of ruin and destruction.

4. In a sinful world, Noah has opted to live a life on God's terms, by keeping faithful relationship with God and others in the world.

5. God's decision to destroy animal lives along with the wicked human race indicates the tragic effect of human sin on all creation.

6. God's instructions to Noah concerning the ark, his family, and the animals indicate God's plan to give creation a new beginning.

WEEK 5, DAY 4

The Flood Story and the Story of God

If you have a study Bible, it may have references in a margin, a middle column, or footnotes that point to other biblical texts. You may find it helpful in understanding how the whole story of God ties together to look up some of those other scriptures from time to time. Whenever we read a biblical text, it is important to ask how the particular text we're reading relates to the rest of the Bible. The flood story, like all other stories in the Bible, has an integral place in the story of the God.

Let's consider some of the biblical passages that are directly or indirectly related to this story or its themes. **In the space given below, write a short summary of how various elements of the flood story are reflected in each passage.**

Genesis 8:21

Human sin resulted in God's curse on the ground. The devastating effect of this curse is
evident in the destruction caused by the flood. God's inner resolve in this verse implies that the
post-flood world can depend on God's blessing for its future, though humans have become evil (see
Genesis 1:22, 28).

1 Samuel 15:11

_____

_____

_____

_____

_____

Psalm 14:1–3

_____

_____

_____

_____

_____

Jeremiah 17:9–10

Jeremiah describes the human heart as totally corrupt, unable to be cured by any human remedy. Though the deceitfulness of the human heart is hidden from others, God has intimate knowledge of the thinking and actions of all humans, and God deals with them accordingly.

Hosea 4:1–3

The prophet Hosea describes here the destructive effect of the sin of God's covenant people on the rest of creation: the land and its inhabitants, the animals of the field, the birds in the sky, and fish in the sea.

Romans 8:18–21

Paul asserts here that human sin affected all non-human creation's capacity to fulfill its role in God's created order, and caused its bondage to ruin. However, he also expresses his hope that creation will be set free to share in the glorious freedom from death and decay that the children of God will enjoy in the world to come.

1 Peter 3:20–21

2 Peter 2:5, 9

WEEK 5, DAY 5

Genesis and Our World Today

When we enter into the narrative of Genesis 6:5–22, the story becomes the lens through which we see ourselves, our world, and God's action in our world today.

1. What does the flood story say to us about ourselves, our world, and God's action in our world today?

God is actively engaged in the affairs of creation. All human actions are subject to divine scrutiny and assessment. We live in a world dominated by the power of sin; wickedness and violence increase in our world at an alarming rate. Sinfulness of the heart is a reality found in all humans of all age levels in our world. Our sinful actions cause grief to God's heart.

Following the above example, answer these questions about how we can understand ourselves, our world, and God's action in our world today.

2. How do you think God judges human sin in our world today?

_____

_____

_____

_____

_____

3. How have you received God's grace in your life?

_____

_____

_____

_____

_____

4. Give one example of the devastating effect of human sin on God's creation in our world today.

_____

_____

_____

_____

_____

5. Though God's judgment of human sin is at work in our world, God continues to care for creation. What is an example you see of this in our world today?

_____

_____

_____

_____

_____

Invitation and Response

God's Word always invites a response. Think about the way the Genesis account of the flood speaks to us today. How does the story invite us to respond?

_____

_____

_____

_____

_____

_____

_____

_____

_____

_____

_____

God's decision in the Noah story to destroy animal lives along with the wicked human race indicates the tragic effect of human sin on all creation.

GENESIS 8:15–9:11

In this section, we find some key aspects of the creation story from Genesis 1:1–2:3. God's judgment in bringing the flood devastates the earth. After the receding of the floodwaters (8:3–5), God begins the work of re-creating the earth and humanity through Noah and his sons. In 8:15–9:11, we find the foundations of God's renewed relationship with the world and humanity. Noah is portrayed in this story as a new Adam, the father of God's re-created humanity after the flood.

The post-flood world and humanity, however, are not the same as those we find in Genesis 1–2. Evil has become a reality in God's good creation. However, God decides to remain in relationship with creation. Moreover, God sets the rules for relationships within creation. In our story, the post-flood world also receives God's original creation mandate and blessings (1:28).

WEEK 6, DAY 1

Listen to the story in Genesis 8:15–9:11 by reading it aloud several times until you become familiar with its verses, words, and phrases. Enjoy the experience of imagining the story in your mind, picturing each event as it unfolds.

WEEK 6, DAY 2
GENESIS 8:15-9:11

The Setting

God's decision to bring the judgment of the floodwaters and the subsequent destruction of the earth and all human and animal life—except those in the ark that Noah built—is the immediate setting of the story of Genesis 8:15-9:11. As we have seen in our previous study, God's decision is not sudden and arbitrary. It is the outcome of God's ongoing evaluation of the increase of human wickedness in the world, beginning in the garden of Eden.

The detailed story of the flood is the focus of Genesis chapters 6-8. Noah follows the instructions God gave him and makes preparations for the escape from the floodwaters. After he and his family and the animals enter the ark, the floodwaters come on the earth. Rain falls continuously for forty days, resulting in a massive flood that rises above the mountains.

God's remembrance of Noah and the promise to establish a covenant with him prompt God to send a wind to cause the water to recede. The ark comes to rest on the mountains of Ararat on the 150th day of the flood. The receding of the water continues until the earth is completely dry. By taking into account the dates given in the flood story, scholars estimate that Noah and his family were in the ark for 365 days.

The Plot

Let's now look at how the writer organizes the story of Genesis 8:15-9:11. The plot will become clear when we examine the various parts of this story, which we will divide into four paragraphs, based on the transitions we notice. Let's examine each of those four paragraphs. **Below, write down next to each grouping of verses the main event or theme those verses report (follow the pattern provided for 8:15-19, 20-22).**

1. Genesis 8:15-19
Noah obeys God's command to come out of the ark with his family and the animals.

2. Genesis 8:20-22
God accepts Noah's offerings and promises to sustain creation even though humans have become evil.

3. Genesis 9:1–7

_____

_____

_____

_____

_____

_____

4. Genesis 9:8–11

_____

_____

_____

_____

_____

_____

WORD STUDY NOTES #1

[1] The description of the animals as "one kind after another" literally means in Hebrew "by their families," a term that describes human relationship in the Old Testament.

WORD STUDY NOTES #2

[1] We do not know the number of animals and birds Noah sacrifices; we can assume the group includes the traditional kinds of animals used for sacrifices, such as oxen, sheep, goats, and a number of birds. Considering the number of animals in the ark, it would be a significant offering. Burnt offering in the Israelite worship system (developed much later than the setting of this story) symbolizes the worshiper's total commitment and consecration to God. It consists of burning the entire animal on the altar.

[2] God's smelling is an example of anthropomorphism in the Old Testament (a description of God using the language of human experience).

[3] "The LORD said in his heart" refers to God's inner resolution, which is stated here as a promise.

[4] "Curse" here may be a reference to the curse on the ground in Genesis 3:17, since 8:21 says, "Never again will I curse the ground."

WEEK 6, DAY 3

What's Happening in the Story?

As we notice certain circumstances in the story, we will begin to see how they are similar to or different from the realities of our world. The story will become the lens through which we see the world in which we live today. In our study today, you may encounter words and/or phrases that are unfamiliar to you. Some of the particular words and translation choices for them have been explained in more detail in the **Word Study Notes**. If you are interested in even more help or detail, you can supplement this study with a Bible dictionary or other Bible study resource.

1. Genesis 8:15–19

When the floodwaters recede and the earth is completely dry, God asks Noah to come out with his family and all the animals he took with him into the ark. All who entered the ark by following God's instructions (see 6:17–21) were kept safe by God when the floodwaters destroyed all life on the earth. By including animals among the occupants of the ark, God has planned for the continuation of animal life on the earth after the flood. The animals are to be released for the purpose of fulfilling God's creational plan to multiply and increase in number on the earth (see the blessing statement in 1:22). Noah obeys God's command; he and his family and all the animals come out of the ark. The repetition of the list of the ark's occupants (vv. 18–19) is intended to emphasize that none remain behind in the ark.[1]

2. Genesis 8:20–22

Noah expresses gratitude to God by building an altar and offering some members of all clean animals and birds that came out of the ark as burnt offerings.[1] The metaphor of God's smelling of the pleasing aroma indicates that God is delighted with Noah's offering.[2] In response to Noah's commitment and loyalty, God promises to put an end to the curse on the earth.[3] Curse will no longer be the way of God's relationship to the earth.[4] What is being implied here is God's commitment to return to blessing as the way God relates to creation. God recognizes that evil remains the human condition even after the flood. Once again, we find here God's evaluation of the human heart as corrupted by evil from childhood (see 6:5). God also promises not to destroy creation again even though humans will continue in their sinful condition. We find here a clear expression of God's grace extended to creation. God's promise also includes the preservation of the agricultural cycle, climate, seasons, and the rhythm of day and night that are necessary for creation's continued existence.

Practice the above pattern to write a summary description of the world and reality that is portrayed in Genesis 9:1–7.

3. Genesis 9:1–7[1, 2]

_____

_____

_____

_____

_____

_____

_____

_____

4. Genesis 9:8–11[1]

_____

_____

_____

_____

_____

_____

_____

_____

WORD STUDY NOTES #3

[1] The description of the animals' "fear and dread" of humans and the declaration that animals are "given into" human hands indicate the tragic consequence of human sin; these phrases are elsewhere used in a military context (see Deuteronomy 11:25; 20:13).

[2] The prohibition "you must not eat meat that has its lifeblood still in it" emphasizes the ancient Israelites' religious belief that "the life of every creature is its blood" (see Leviticus 17:14). So someone eating meat with blood in it is eating life. Since God is the Creator of life, eating meat with blood in it is considered to be a total disregard for the Creator of life. God's regard for humans as created in God's image continues even after God's evaluation of the human condition as evil.

WORD STUDY NOTES #4

[1] The term "covenant" (*berit*) conveys the idea of a legal agreement through which a formal relationship is established between two parties. Though in ancient times, the covenant involved the agreement of both parties, here it is a unilateral agreement made by God and characterized by God's promise. This is the first record of God's covenant that we find in the Bible.

Discoveries

Let's summarize some our discoveries from Genesis 8:15–9:11.

1. By preserving Noah and his family and various kinds of animals in the ark, God makes provisions for the re-creation and repopulation of the earth and its human and animal inhabitants after the devastation of the flood.

2. When Noah comes out of the ark with his family as directed by God, he builds an altar and worships God.

3. God promises that curse will no longer be the way of God's relationship to the earth.

4. God promises to sustain the natural cycles necessary for the continued existence of creation.

5. God blesses Noah and his sons and commands them to fulfill God's creation mandate by multiplying and populating the earth.

6. God grants humans permission to include meat in their diet, with the condition that they do not eat meat with blood remaining in it.

7. God declares that if a human life is taken, the killer will suffer the same fate by humans. The high value of humans as created in and reflecting God's image is God's rationale for capital punishment.

8. God establishes a covenant with Noah, his sons, and their future descendants, as well as with all the animals on the earth.

9. God promises to never again destroy the earth and its creatures by a flood.

WEEK 6, DAY 4

The Post-Flood Covenant Story and the Story of God

If you have a study Bible, it may have references in a margin, a middle column, or footnotes that point to other biblical texts. You may find it helpful in understanding how the whole story of God ties together to look up some of those other scriptures from time to time. Whenever we read a biblical text, it is important to ask how the particular text we're reading relates to the rest of the Bible. Though the specifics of the story found in Genesis 8:15–9:11 are not mentioned directly elsewhere in the Bible, we find several of the same themes and ideas in a number of other passages. **In the space given below, write a short summary of how some of the themes from Genesis 8:15–9:11 are utilized in each passage.**

Exodus 21:12, 14, 28; Leviticus 24:17

_____

_____

_____

_____

Leviticus 1:3–9

The Israelites' sacrificial system regards a burnt offering as an aroma pleasing to the Lord.

Leviticus 17:10–14; Deuteronomy 12:23

_____

_____

_____

_____

Leviticus 26:31

God warns the Israelites that their disobedient and hostile attitude toward him will prompt him

to take no delight in the pleasing aroma of their offerings.

1 Samuel 14:31–34

_____
_____
_____
_____
_____
_____

Isaiah 54:9

_____
_____
_____
_____
_____
_____

2 Corinthians 2:15

_____
_____
_____
_____
_____
_____

WEEK 6, DAY 5

Genesis and Our World Today

When we enter into the intriguing narrative of Genesis 8:15–9:11, the story becomes the lens through which we see ourselves, our world, and God's action in our world today.

1. What does the Genesis story of the post-flood covenant say to us about ourselves, our world, and God's actions in our lives today?

We live in a world of human sin and God's judgment, but we also experience God's commitment

to bless creation. God's concern for the future of creation includes concern for the well-being of

both animals and human beings. We see evidence of God's commitment to preserve creation in the

regular and steady seasonal cycles of the year and in the rhythm of day and night. God's faithful

people in the world express their gratitude to God for their salvation through faithful acts of worship.

Following the above example, answer these questions about how we can understand ourselves, our world, and God's action in our world today.

2. What does Genesis 9:1 say to us about the way God blesses humanity today?

_____

_____

_____

_____

_____

_____

3. How do you characterize human-animal interactions today?

_____

_____

_____

_____

_____

_____

4. How would you reconcile the statement about animals' fear and dread of humans in Genesis 9:2 with God's command to be caretakers of the animal world in 1:28?

_____

_____

_____

_____

_____

5. What value do human communities place on human lives?

_____

_____

_____

_____

_____

6. How do you reconcile God's promise to preserve the natural cycles with the environmental disasters that humans cause in our industrial world today?

_____

_____

_____

_____

_____

Invitation and Response

God's Word always invites a response. Think about the way the Genesis account of creation speaks to us today. How does the story invite us to respond?

_____

_____

_____

_____

_____

95

We see evidence of
God's commitment
to preserve creation
in the regular and
steady seasonal
cycles of the year
and in the rhythm
of day and night.

GENESIS 11:1–9

A key emphasis of Genesis 11:1–9 is the scattering of the descendants of Noah over the face of the earth by God. However, the genealogical account in chapter 10 presents the identity of different family, language, and nation groups that originated from the three sons of Noah and their geographical locations. This account offers a picture of the natural growth and geographical distribution of Noah's descendants over the earth after the flood (see 10:32). The story of 11:1–9 actually explains what caused the growth and development of Noah's descendants into various language and national groups in different geographical regions. Thus, chronologically, the story of 11:1–9 precedes the genealogy of chapter 10.

Scholars see in the "tower that reaches to the heavens" a reflection of the stepped, tower-like structures known as *ziggurats* of the ancient Mesopotamians. The remains of many such towers, which were made—some large and some small—of mud bricks, still exist in southern Mesopotamia. One such *ziggurat* was named "Temple of the Stairway to Pure Heaven." Ancient Mesopotamians regarded these towers as the stairways from earth to heaven and their tops as the gateways to heaven.

97

WEEK 7, DAY 1

Listen to the story in Genesis 11:1–9 by reading it aloud several times until you become familiar with its verses, words, and phrases. Enjoy the experience of imagining the story in your mind, picturing each event as it unfolds.

WEEK 7, DAY 2
GENESIS 11:1–9

The Setting

We have been following the story of God, which begins in the Bible with the story of creation. We saw in Genesis 3 how the humans created in God's image disobey God's command, disrupting their relationships with God, with other humans, and with the rest of creation. The story of Cain in Genesis 4 shows how violence becomes part of the story of humankind. As humans increase and multiply, violence and wickedness also increase on the earth (5:1–6:5).

In the genealogy of Adam, Enoch is only one who walks faithfully with God (5:21–24). The story of the marriage of "the sons of God" and "the daughters of humans" (6:1–4) shows sin becoming cosmic in scope and breaking down the boundary between heaven and earth. The continued growth of violence and wickedness on the earth causes God to regret creating humans.

In grief and agony, God sends as judgment a catastrophic flood that destroys all human and nonhuman life on the earth. However, in the midst of the judgment, God preserves Noah and his family and some animals so that creation can have a future after it suffers destruction.

This is the setting in which we find story of the Tower of Babel in Genesis 11:1–9. Noah's descendants are introduced in this story as those who have chosen a way of life different from that of their ancestor, who walked faithfully with God.

The Tower of Babel story is followed by a brief sketch of the family line of Shem, one of the three sons of Noah, through his son Arphaxad; the genealogy ends with the family line of Terah, the father of Abram (11:10–30). (The extended family line of Shem is found in 10:21–31).

Genesis 11:31–32 presents the departure of Terah and his family from Ur of the Chaldeans (southern Mesopotamia), with Canaan as their destination. By placing this story in chapter 11, the writer may have intended to link the journey of Terah and his family to the migration from Babel (11:9).

The Plot

The plot will become clear when we examine the various parts of this story. For the purpose of our study, we will divide Genesis 11:1–9 into five smaller groupings of verses based on the transitions we notice in them. Let's examine each of those five paragraphs. Write down next to each grouping of verses the main event or theme those verses report (follow the pattern provided for vv. 1–2, 3–4, and 5–7).

1. Genesis 11:1–2

These verses describe the migration and settlement of the human community that spoke only one language.

2. Genesis 11:3–4

The human community decides to build a city to make a name for themselves so they will not be scattered over the face of the earth.

3. Genesis 11:5–7

God decides to prevent this and any future projects by confusing the community's language, which is the key to their unity.

4. Genesis 11:8

5. Genesis 11:9

WEEK 7, DAY 3

What's Happening in the Story?

As we notice certain circumstances in the story, we will begin to see how they are similar to or different from the realities of our world. The story, in other words, will become the lens through which we see the world in which we live today. In our study today, you may encounter words and/or phrases that are unfamiliar to you. Some of the particular words and translation choices for them have been explained in more detail in the **Word Study Notes**. If you are interested in even more help or detail, you can supplement this study with a Bible dictionary or other Bible study resource.

1. Genesis 11:1–2

Verse 1 portrays the reality that exists after the flood; the human community on earth[1] speaks the same language and shares a common vocabulary. This relatively small group of people, who are most likely tent dwellers, migrate to the east and settle in the land of Shinar.

2. Genesis 11:3–4

The settled human community decides together to make bricks and bake them in order to build a city for themselves with bricks and tar. Their joint decision also includes the making of a tower with its top reaching to the heavens.[1] The decision to build a city and a tower is motivated by their desire for greatness in the world.[2] They think their fame and greatness will keep them together as one unified people in one place; they express their concern that if they fail to make a name for themselves, they will be scattered over the face of the earth.[3]

WORD STUDY NOTES #1

[1] The phrase "the whole world" (or the whole earth) could also mean the whole land or region. The Hebrew word here (*'erets*) more often refers to "land" or a "region" in the Old Testament.

WORD STUDY NOTES #2

[1] The tower with its top reaching the heavens indicates either a fortified city tower for protection or a temple tower for easy access to the heavens. We do not need to read "a tower that reaches to the heavens" literally (see Deuteronomy 1:28). It is most likely the people's prideful boasting of the greatness they hope to achieve through the city and the tower.

[2] "Make a name for ourselves" indicates the people's decision to secure their fame and future by their own effort. They do not see God's blessing as the source of their reputation in the world (see God's promise in Genesis 12:2).

[3] The people's resistance to being scattered indicates their resistance to both the creation mandate and the mandate God gave to Noah and his sons (see Genesis 1:28; 9:1).

WORD STUDY NOTES #3

[1] Genesis 1:26 also utilizes the first-person-plural form when God speaks. Though scholars suggest various possibilities, we regard "us" in verse 7 as the plural of God's majesty.

[2] It is important to note here that God's action is directed against a human community that has defiantly resisted God's creational plan. God is not condemning the human effort to build cities or to be in unity. God's action is directed against a community that seeks self-preservation through its isolationist agenda and freedom from its responsibility to God and the rest of creation.

WORD STUDY NOTES #5

[1] The literal meaning of *Babel* is "gate of god." This word is a play on the verb *balal* ("to confuse") found in verses 7 and 9. "Babel" refers to the city of Babylon.

3. Genesis 11:5–7

Verse 5 portrays God's coming down from heaven "to see" the building project of the people. God's action here implies God's decision to conduct a thorough inquiry of what the people are doing. God's coming down also indicates that, even though the people are building a tower that reaches to the heavens, the heavens remain far from their reach. God's inquiry leads God to conclude that humans, through their unified efforts made possible by their common language, have the potential to accomplish anything they plan to do.[1] In verse 7, God responds to the humans' potential by deciding to "go down" to the earth and confuse their language, which will inevitably confuse their unified efforts.[2]

Practice the above pattern to write a summary description of the world and reality that is portrayed in verses 8 and 9.

4. Genesis 11:8

_____

_____

_____

_____

_____

5. Genesis 11:9[1]

_____

_____

_____

_____

_____

Discoveries

Let's summarize our discoveries from Genesis 11:1–9.

1. Members of the human community once spoke the same language and shared a common vocabulary.

2. The settled human community decided to build a city with a tower in order to establish their greatness in the world.

3. The motivation behind the city-building was their determination to stay in one place and not be a people spread throughout the world, which displays post-flood humanity's resistance to the mandate God gave them to populate the earth.

4. God's decision to confuse their language and scatter them brought an end to the people's united endeavor to make a name for themselves.

5. The name Babel ("confusion") indicates the futility of humans' attempt to make a name for themselves by their own efforts and resistance to God's plan for them.

6. Though Noah's descendants resisted God's mandate to fill the earth, God fulfilled the mandate through the judgment of their scattering.

7. A clear implication of this story is that diversity is God's creational intent for human beings. In this story, God promotes diversity by destroying humans' unified efforts to resist God's plan for them.

WEEK 7, DAY 4

The Tower of Babel Story and the Story of God

Though we do not find any direct reference to the Tower of Babel incident elsewhere in the Bible, it—like all other stories in the Bible—has an integral place in the story of God. The themes of human pride and rebellion against God's creational plan are found in several places in the Bible in a variety of contexts. We also find in the story of God, God's efforts to gather the human community together and unify them so that they may once again serve their creational purpose and become mediators of God's blessings on the earth. Let's consider some of the passages that echo different concerns expressed in this story.

Genesis 1:28; 9:1

In both passages, God directs human beings to be fruitful, multiply, and fill the earth. These passages make clear God's mandate to human beings to participate in his creational intent for them.

Genesis 10:1–32

The geographical dispersion of the descendants of Noah and the development of various language groups in this chapter show the outcome of God's scattering of the Tower of Babel community (11:8-9).

Genesis 11:31

The journey of Terah and his family from Ur of the Chaldeans (southern Mesopotamia) could be associated with the migration of the scattered humanity from Babel/Babylon.

Genesis 12:1–3

Here we find the beginning of God's gathering activity of dispersed humanity. God calls Abram, a member of the scattered human family, to follow God's commands and become a blessing to "all peoples on earth" (Genesis 12:1-3).

Genesis 12:2

God's promise to make Abraham's name "great" shows that God alone can make the name of a person or a group of people or a nation great in the world. This promise stands in stark contrast to the plans of the Tower of Babel community to make a name for themselves through their city-building project.

In the space given below, write down a short summary of how different concerns expressed in the Tower of Babel story are echoed in the following passages.

Genesis 18:20–21

_____

_____

_____

_____

_____

Genesis 28:16–17

_____

_____

_____

_____

_____

Proverbs 8:13; 11:2; 16:18

_____

_____

_____

_____

_____

Hosea 5:5

_____

_____

_____

_____

_____

Obadiah 3

_____
_____
_____
_____
_____

Luke 1:51

_____
_____
_____
_____
_____

We find in the Gospels another kind of God's scattering activity.

Matthew 28:18–20

_____
_____
_____
_____
_____

The message of the gospel of Jesus Christ brings unity in the midst of diversity. How would you relate the events on the day of Pentecost to the Tower of Babel incident?

Acts 2:1–12

_____
_____
_____
_____
_____

Describe the scattering of the church in Acts 8:1 and its outcome, based on your reading of the Book of Acts.

_____

_____

_____

_____

_____

What does the apostle Paul say about the goal of the church's unity and diversity in Ephesians 4:1–13?

_____

_____

_____

_____

_____

WEEK 7, DAY 5

Genesis and Our World Today

When we enter into the intriguing narrative of Genesis 11:1–9, the story becomes the lens through which we see ourselves, our world, and God's action in our world today.

1. What does the Tower of Babel story say to us about ourselves, our world, and God's action in our world today?

We also live in a world where some groups promote isolationism and protectionism, motivated their

fear of others and concern for their self-preservation. Nations, political leaders, ideological groups,

and individuals continue to strive to make a name for themselves in our world. Describe below your

observation of how this is being done in our world:

2. The fear of being "scattered over the face of the earth" in our day could be the concern over the potential loss of a group's cultural and geographical identity. What do some groups or people do in our day to preserve their cultural or ethnic identities?

3. What do you observe about diversity in God's creation?

4. What do you observe about the level of diversity in your community or workplace?

_____

_____

_____

_____

_____

5. What is your observation of the some of the positive outcomes resulting from human unity in our world today?

_____

_____

_____

_____

_____

6. What is your observation of unity and diversity in the church today?

_____

109

_____

_____

_____

_____

7. What does this story say about the need for both diversity *and* unity among God's people to promote God's plans and purposes for the world?

_____

_____

_____

_____

_____

Invitation and Response

God's Word always invites a response. Think about the way the Genesis account of creation speaks to us today. How does the story invite us to respond?

_____

_____

_____

_____

_____

_____

_____

_____

_____

_____

_____

_____

_____

_____

_____

_____

_____

_____

_____

_____

Diversity is God's
creational intent
for human beings.